W9-CNA-870

Fortune-Telling

FORTUNE TELLING

Elaine Landau

The Millbrook Press ❑ *Brookfield, Connecticut*
Mysteries of Science

Photographs courtesy of Photo Researchers: pp. 8 (© Spencer Grant), 12 (© Oscar Burriel/Latin Stock/Science Photo Library), 18 (© Chris Marona), 35 (© Laurence Gartel/Science Source); Bettmann Archive: pp. 15, 23, 41; New York Public Library Picture Collection: pp. 20, 37; The Image Works: p. 25 (© John Eastcott/Yva Momatiuk); Scala/Art Resource, NY: p. 28; Rosanna Rogers: p. 30; North Wind Picture Archives: p. 32; © Devon Cass: p. 43.

Library of Congress Cataloging-in-Publication Data
Landau, Elaine.
Fortune-telling / by Elaine Landau.
p.   cm. — (Mysteries of science)
Includes bibliographical references and index.
Summary: Explores palmistry, tarot card reading, crystal gazing, and other techniques that purport to foretell the future.
ISBN 0-7613-0013-9
1. Fortune-telling—Juvenile literature. [1. Fortune telling.]
I. Title. II. Series: Landau, Elaine. Mysteries of science.
BF1861.L45 1996 133.3—dc20 95-47687 CIP AC

Cover illustration and design
by Anne Canevari Green

Contents

For My Son, Michael Brent Pearl,
who has brought us
nothing but love and good fortune.

Introduction

PSYCHIC READINGS BY GENA
read the flyer given out by a dark-haired
boy on a New York City street corner.
"Do you have problems with the law, health,
marriage, and success?" it continued.
"Come see this gifted lady and let her
solve your problems today."

The "gifted lady" described in the flyer
also promised "to show you how she can
take away suffering, sickness, and bad luck
from your home and body."[1]

Gena, like thousands of other fortune-tellers, claims to accomplish these feats by reading palms and tarot cards. Other fortune-tellers rely on crystal balls and other devices. Although Gena practices her craft in New York City, fortune-tellers can be found in every major U.S. city as well as in numerous smaller towns.

In some instances these individuals have been remarkably convincing. Many of their clients report that fortune-tellers both accurately predicted future events in their lives and offered valuable advice. But is it possible to see someone's future by reading a palm, a deck of cards, or looking into a crystal ball?

This book explores the mystical arts of palmistry (reading palms), tarot card reading, crystal gazing, and other techniques of fortune-telling that have fascinated people since ancient times. It answers as well as raises some intriguing questions.

The Crystal Ball

"I'll look into my crystal ball and see your future," a fortune-teller told a young female client. The woman had come to the fortune-teller hoping to learn what lay ahead.

She didn't realize that the crystal gazer she saw was actually practicing a centuries-old art known as scrying.

The term scrying comes from the English word "descry," which means "to discover."

A smooth, clear object such as a crystal ball can indeed appear mysterious. Little drops of water on the ball were bathed in red and green light to create this eerie effect.

In scrying, an individual attempts to see the future by concentrating or focusing on a smooth, clear object. Besides crystal balls, a wide assortment of items have been used for this purpose. Through the years these have included sparkling clear lakes, goblets (rounded long-stemmed glasses) of water, doorknobs, mirrors, shiny smooth jewelry pieces, soap bubbles, or even an unworn patent leather shoe. Scryers (those who practice this art) argue that the object used is not important. It merely serves as a device on which to focus—enabling them to get in touch with their ability to see the future.

Among the best-known crystal gazers of the late nineteenth century was an Englishwoman named Nell St. John Montague. The daughter of a major general in the British army, Montague was born in India, where her father was stationed just before the turn of the century. As a small child she was cared for by an Indian nanny, who gave her a beautiful crystal ball to play with. The ball was among the young girl's favorite possessions. She loved looking into it and carried it with her wherever she went.

However, one day as she gazed into her ball, the crystal suddenly became cloudy. Montague felt as if the ball were somehow fading away. In its place "a thick black mist" appeared before her.[1] Within the dark haze, Nell St. John Montague had a frightening vision. She saw her mother reaching for a blue dressing gown that lay folded on the bed. But just as her mother went to pick up the garment, a deadly cobra came out from under it.

Terrified by the sight, young Nell ran to see if her mother was all right. Hoping to comfort her daughter, she took Nell and a male servant to the bedroom to inspect the dressing gown. The gown was on the bed just as it was in the vision. But to their horror, when the servant lifted it, a snake was posed to strike beneath it.

After that unsettling incident, Nell St. John Montague's parents believed their daughter had a special talent. And as she grew older, she frequently proved they were right. Once, when a naval officer asked her to tell his fortune, she saw a particularly disturbing scene in the crystal. The ball showed several injured women lying on the floor. Their clothes were torn, and there was blood everywhere.

Montague was shocked by the violent image. She wondered if the women were dead. And if they were, was the man before her their murderer? If she told him what she'd seen, Montague thought he might kill her as well. But despite the possible personal risk, she decided to tell the truth.

As it turned out, the naval officer wrote to her a year later to say that the vision had come true. Following a disastrous earthquake, his ship was among those assigned to transport the injured to safety. During that mission the women who had appeared in the crystal ball were brought on board his vessel. The scene was exactly as Montague described it on the day she told his fortune.

Crystal gazing continues today and those who practice this ancient art are often quite specific about the tools they need. Most prefer a ball of natural crystal about 4 to 5 inches (10 to 13 centimeters) wide. However, a less expensive glass ball of the same size is also acceptable. In addition, proper maintenance of the crystal is important. Scryers suggest that crystal balls be kept in a cool dark place and not be frequently moved or exposed to temperature changes. The ball should also be periodically wiped with a soft velvet cloth. It's important that the crystal not have any scratches, smudges, or marks on it that could distract the user.

In addition to keeping the ball spotless, some scryers attempt to purify their minds and bodies prior to using the

This crystal gazer holds his cupped hands the recommended distance from the ball. Both the astrological signs on his clothing and his gold earrings complete the picture of a well-equipped fortune-teller.

crystal. This may involve praying and thinking only pure thoughts for several days beforehand. Numerous scryers also fast or just eat organic (naturally grown) foods.

For best results, crystal gazing should be done in a dimly lit room. The ball should rest on a thick dark cloth to reduce any reflections that might appear in the glass. The crystal gazer may also glide his or her hands just above the ball to become in touch with his or her inner power.

Those who practice this art report that after steadily gazing at the crystal for several minutes, colorful swirling clouds usually appear within it. Supposedly, these clouds give way to images revealing the inquirer's (the person having his fortune told) future. If only clouds are seen in the ball, the scryer may still be able to glean some information from the cloud colors. These colors are said to have the following meanings:

White: good things lie ahead

Black: sadness and disappointment are in
the inquirer's future

Red, Yellow, and Orange: the inquirer
will experience an undesirable occurrence

While predictions based on colors and images may sound fascinating, many people doubt that crystal gazers have any genuine ability. It's been suggested that scryers really don't interpret images seen in the crystal. Instead they may actually pick up subtle cues from the clients who seek them out. It might be something the person said or the way he or she dressed, sat, or smiled. In any case, the scryer may unknowingly mix this information with what he or she believes appears in the crystal ball. Anyone who sees a crystal gazer, therefore, does so because of his or her personal belief in the process.

Palmistry

Can our hands reveal our destiny?

People in various places throughout
the world have tried to find this
out for thousands of years.

Individuals who claim to have
the ability to read people's palms
are called palmists.

Palm reading was considered a science in ancient times, but in today's world many palmists have taken on the trappings of crystal gazers and other less scientific members of the fortune-telling world.

Palmists look at the shape of a person's hands as well as the various lines crossing the palms. They believe that the left hand shows the individual's inner potential or ability. These are qualities the person is born with and may or may not have already developed. Palmists say that the right hand reveals the opportunities available to the person throughout his or her life.

Palm readers think that everyone's hands fall into one of four basic types. They say that each of the following hand types reflects distinct personality traits:

The Air Hand: People with air hands have square palms and long graceful fingers. They tend not to accept facts unquestioningly and do not hesitate to express their thoughts and feelings. An air hand person also enjoys hearing new ideas and meeting people. Those with air hands frequently become teachers, lawyers, and authors.

The Earth Hand: Someone with earth hands has square palms and short fingers. These individuals are usually athletic and enjoy a number of different sports. Earth hand people frequently work at occupations requiring a good deal of activity. They become gym instructors and coaches as well as construction workers or farmers.

The Water Hand: This type of hand is characterized by a rectangular palm and long fingers. Water hand people are said to be calm, thoughtful, and often quite creative. They frequently become scientists, researchers, or artists.

The Fire Hand: Individuals with fire hands have rectangular palms and short fingers. They are generally quick thinking, outgoing, and willing to take chances. Such people often find careers in the entertainment industry, in public relations, or in law enforcement.

Besides the overall hand shape, palm readers also look at the various mounds (raised areas) of the palm as well as the person's thumb and fingertip shapes. However, they pay special attention to the various lines crossing the palm. The lines listed below are among those that are thought to be especially revealing:

The Life Line: The life line is easy to identify. Starting between the thumb and the index finger, it runs down the side of the palm outlining the thumb's base. A lengthy, clearly defined life line supposedly indicates a person will enjoy a long, healthy, vital life.

However, a short life line doesn't necessarily mean an early death. Besides possibly indicating the length of some-

A fifteenth-century palmistry book shows (clockwise from upper left) the hand of an "Avaricious and Thoughtless Man," a "Stubborn and Iniquitous Man," an "Irascible and Evil Man," and the wrist of a "Woman Unsuited for Motherhood."

one's life, this line supposedly also shows an individual's life force—the energy and enthusiasm characteristic of his or her existence. A short but deeply marked life line is often found on people who meet life's challenges courageously and effectively. Small lines crossing the life line show stress and problems. But an actual break in the line may be a major accident, illness, or dramatic life-style change.

The Head Line: The head line supposedly reveals a person's intellect or mental ability as well as how he or she approaches life. Starting between the thumb and index fingers, it crosses the palm horizontally (widthwise). A straight deeply marked head line indicates an intelligent person with an excellent memory.

In doing a reading, palmists note precisely where the head line begins. If the head line is joined with the life line at its start, the person is likely to be cautious and self-controlled. Such precise and efficient individuals usually put reason before emotion. However, someone whose head line is not joined with his or her life line is thought to be the opposite. These people are generally adventurous and fun loving.

The Heart Line: The heart line reflects the person's kindness and understanding as well as how he or she will fare in romance. Beginning under either the index or middle finger, the heart line horizontally crosses the palm directly above

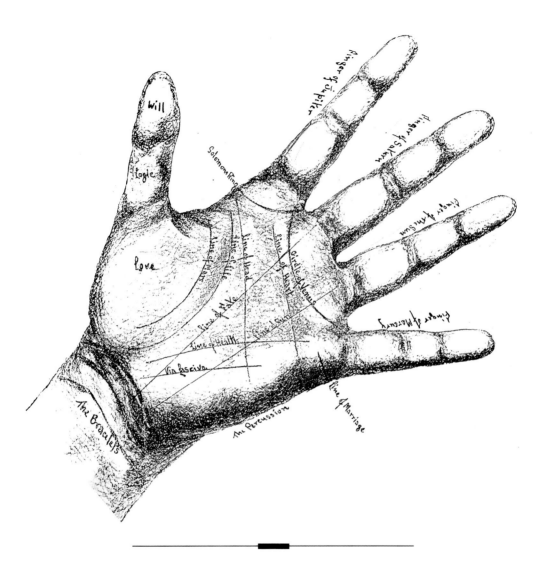

A map of the hand showing the various lines and fleshy portions that palmists claim can expose a person's character or foretell that person's future.

the head line. Palmists believe that people who have very strong deep heart lines are capable of boundless warmth and generosity.

People whose heart line begins under the index finger are likely to have a stable and fulfilling love life. However, people whose heart lines start closer to the middle finger may be quick to give their hearts away and are likely to be disappointed in love.

The Fate Line: Starting near the wrist, the fate line runs straight up the palm toward the middle finger. When this line appears to be particularly deep and strong, forces beyond the person's control are thought to greatly affect that individual's life.

Small lines crossing the fate line supposedly reveal the times when fate plays a major role. Someone who has strong life, head, and heart lines but a faint fate line is believed to largely shape his or her own future.

Palmists think that events dictated by the fate line cannot be altered. However, some insist that knowing about these incidents in advance can help a person handle his or her destiny.

As one fortune-teller described the process: "The point is not to predict things, it's to help people deal with their lives in a better way."[1]

This might mean making the most of a unique opportunity or being open to new ways of doing things if an undesirable change occurs.

*Skeptics claim that palm readers cleverly "read" physical
signs such as muscular spasms or perspiration that lead them
to accurate revelations about their client's past or future.*

Those who question this art argue that palmistry is hardly a dependable source of information. The meanings attached to various lines, markings, and hand shapes may differ depending on where the palm reader is from. As in crystal gazing, it's also difficult to know if the fortune-teller is actually responding to hints from the inquirer rather than what is revealed in the palm.

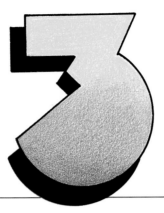

Tarot Cards

The tarot is a deck of seventy-eight strange and often hauntingly beautiful cards.

Thought to be the forerunners of modern-day playing cards, some believe that their name comes from the ancient Hindu word "taru," meaning "pack of cards."

Tarot card readers claim to interpret the symbols on the cards for answers to everyday questions as well as to see the future.

In addition to the symbols, they stress that the way the cards fall and the relationship between various cards are also important.

Tarot card readings may greatly vary. It's said that "there are as many interpretations of the tarot as there are interpreters [tarot card readers]." [1]

Most people come to a reading with questions about romance, health, career, or travel. Believers in the mystical power of the tarot deck say that predictions can either come true in the near future or years later. That's what happened when Jeff, a fourteen-year-old boy, had his cards read at a carnival. As a child, Jeff had always wanted a dog, but his parents wouldn't hear of it. Yet when Jeff had his cards read, he was told that he'd have a dog. The tarot reader said that the animal would be brown and white and quite frisky. Jeff was thrilled by the idea, but his hopes were dashed when his parents still refused.

As Jeff grew older his yearning for a pet lessened. He didn't even think about a dog again until he was married and learned that he and his wife weren't able to have children. However, they still never got a dog because Jeff's wife found that she was allergic to them.

When his wife died some forty years later, Jeff was too old and ill to look after a pet. The following year he even entered a nursing home. However, the home had a program in which animals were brought to the facility for the residents to enjoy. Jeff was completely taken aback when one day a friendly brown-and-white puppy scampered over to him. After that, the animal remained at his side whenever it was brought to the home. Jeff had nearly forgotten about the tarot card reader's prediction. Yet before he died, he told his friends how it had come true almost sixty-five years later.

Although Jeff became a firm believer in tarot cards, many people remain skeptical. The claims of tarot card readers are not supported by scientific data. In fact, the small amount of research in this area tends to show the opposite. In a jointly conducted study in England and North Carolina in the 1980s volunteers had tarot card readings done without immediately learning the results. Instead, the tarot readers' findings were written up and the study participants were asked to pick the one they thought was theirs. In the vast majority of cases, the volunteers selected the wrong results.

Skeptics therefore argued that the tarot card readings did not actually pertain to the volunteers' lives. As in palmistry and crystal ball gazing, they feel that in face-to-face situations tarot card readers may be influenced by other factors, causing them to adjust their interpretation of the cards.

Modern tarot cards, such as this rendering of Tarot 16, The Tower, *are often handpainted.*

Artist Rosanna Rogers has used mythological characters to help give impressions, and numbers that she says help in timing and in clarifying planetary and astrological sign information.

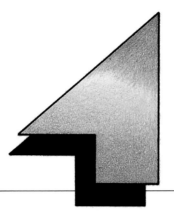

Dice, Numerology, Coins, Tea Leaves

Besides those already discussed, there are numerous other methods used by fortune-tellers to predict the future.

Many are centuries old and no longer common today. Others have both risen and declined in popularity over the years.

Some of the better-known techniques are described briefly in this chapter.

Fortune-telling dates from ancient times. Here an ancient Greek is consulting the Oracle at Delphi, a priestess believed to have the power to foretell the future. The Greeks believed that while the priestess at Delphi was in a trance, the god Apollo spoke through her.

Dice ❑ At times fortune-tellers have used dice to see into their clients' futures. To begin they draw a chalk Sorcerer's Circle—a circle containing two triangles with one placed over the other to form a six-point star. Then using his or her left hand, the fortune-teller shakes three dice and tosses them onto the circle.

How the dice fall is crucial. If two or more dice land outside the circle, the fortune-teller throws the dice again. If the same thing happens a second time, the client is usually told to leave and not return for two to three weeks. The person may also be advised to postpone any major decisions during that time.

But if only one die lands outside the circle, the fortune-teller can proceed. The client's future is supposedly revealed through the number showing on the die.

The meanings attached to the possible different numbers are listed below:

One: The client will enjoy good health and prosperity in the near future and for some time to come.

Two: It would be wise to avoid taking trips for the next two months. The client must also be more considerate of others or suffer the consequences.

Three: Considered a lucky number, a three indicates success in both love and work.

Four: The client will find the ability to overcome seemingly insurmountable obstacles.

Five: Hard times lie ahead, but in the end goodness triumphs.

Six: The client will be successful in romance.

When all the dice fall within the Sorcerer's Circle, the meanings for the various numbers change. In these cases, the fortune-teller adds the numbers shown on the dice and interprets the sum total for the client.

Coins ❑ Coins can also be used as a fortune-telling tool. Ideally, two coins of the same denomination (such as two quarters, two dimes, or two nickels) are used. As with dice, the fortune-teller draws a Sorcerer's Circle (see above) on a flat surface. But before the fortune-teller tosses the coins onto the circle, the client must ask the question that he or she wants answered. If both coins land tails up, the answer is yes. When one coin lands heads up and the other tails up, the answer is still yes—but the occurrence won't come to pass for some time. However, if both coins fall heads up, the answer is no.

Numerology ❑ As with dice (see above), in numerology numbers are used to predict the future. One of the most common forms of numerology centers on the client's date of birth. First the person's birth date is translated into numbers. Therefore if someone were born on June 6, 1986, it would be 6/6/86. Then the numbers are added together like this: $6 + 6 + 8 + 6$, equaling 26. At that point the number is split apart and the digits are added together as follows: $2 + 6 = 8$.

Computers have made a major contribution to figuring out the complex relationship between numbers and the planets.

The final number and its meaning are connected to a particular star or planet that also influences the person's fate, as indicated below:

One—The Sun: The number one is characteristic of a persistent person possessing a great deal of drive and determination. These individuals are likely to do well in school or business.

Two—The Moon: The number two is representative of someone who is friendly and makes others feel at ease. These people enjoy strong family ties as well as lasting friendships.

Three—Jupiter: The number three is characteristic of a precise, efficient, and punctual individual. Such people usually accomplish what they set out to do.

Four—Uranus: The number four indicates someone who copes well with change and is able to do more than one thing at a time. Frequently, these people become trendsetters.

Five—Mercury: The number five reflects a vital, enthusiastic individual. Many find rewarding careers in music or the performing arts.

Six—Venus: The number six is characteristic of a thoughtful and forgiving person who tends to have stable relationships.

Seven—Neptune: The number seven indicates an exceedingly lucky person. These people often win raffles and lotteries.

Eight—Saturn: The number eight is characteristic of a highly intelligent person who prefers working alone to being part of a team. Many are creative thinkers and inventors.

Nine—Mars: The number nine is representative of someone with unusual determination. Such individuals are often persuasive enough to win others over to their side. They frequently become leaders in industry and politics.

The reading of tea leaves was considered an amusing pastime by turn-of-the-century ladies.

Tea Leaf Reading ❏ For thousands of years fortune-tellers known as tea leaf readers have used the leftover particles in a cup of brewed tea to predict the future. They claim that these tea leaf pieces form symbols that represent upcoming events.

Tea leaf readers say that a number of factors influence a "reading." These include precisely where in the cup the symbols appear. Those close to the rim represent events occurring soon, while symbols toward the cup's bottom supposedly show what will happen in the future. The size of the symbol is meaningful as well. Smaller symbols are said to be less important than larger, clearly defined ones.

Tea leaf readers generally prefer a round cup to one with square sides. Any tea with large well-formed leaves may be used, and some tea leaf readers even read coffee grounds.

Although tea leaf reading and some forms of numerology are still frequently practiced by fortune-tellers, the use of dice and coins is rarer. Yet remnants of these techniques remain in our culture. When uncertain about a decision affecting the future, some people flip a coin to decide.

Wishful Thinking v. Reality

While the value of palmistry, tarot card reading, crystal ball gazing, and other methods remains unproven, these practices have their share of believers.

Unfortunately, many have found their faith in fortune-telling to be quite costly. Although some who practice the mystical arts do so in good faith, others attempt to dupe their clients at every opportunity.

That's what an undercover New York City reporter discovered after visiting several fortune-tellers while pretending to be a client. One fortune-teller read both her palm and tarot cards for twenty dollars. After offering the reporter some encouraging news, the fortune-teller pointed out a problem. She said: "You have a dark aura around you. You need spiritual cleansing. There are people around you who are jealous and want to hurt you."[1]

She assured the reporter that she could remove the curse using prayer, crystals, and candles. But this service wasn't included in the twenty-dollar fee already paid. To begin the process, the reporter would have to purchase three candles at a cost of one hundred dollars!

The reporter, who was only writing an article, wasn't taken in by the ploy. However, countless other people have been cheated out of thousands of dollars in similar situations. Fortune-tellers are unlicensed and unregulated by any government agency. And often clients who have lost a good deal of money feel too embarrassed about it to report what happened to the authorities. Patricia Cohen, a spokeswoman for New York City's Department of Consumer Affairs, described what frequently occurs: "Frankly, a lot of people who go to them would not feel free to complain. It would be hard to give them restitution [return their money] if someone said they'd meet the man of their dreams and get married and they didn't."[2]

Considering their questionable predictions and advice, why do many people seek out fortune-tellers? Are we so

*Fortune-tellers have long been known to prey upon
people's natural desire to find love and happiness.*

anxious to know the future that we are willing to believe the unlikely? Or is it because nearly everyone has heard stories about fortune-tellers who were uncannily correct?

One such case involved a young pregnant woman who went to a palmist. She wanted to learn whether she was having a boy or girl and what that child would be when he or she grew up. However, she was doubly disappointed by what she heard. She had wanted a son but was told that she was having a girl. And while she hoped that as an adult her child would enjoy a secure, financially rewarding career, the palm reader said that the girl would become a writer.

The woman tried not think about the predictions. She told herself that the fortune-teller was probably only guessing and that none of it would happen. But she gave birth to a baby girl who, as she grew older, showed a keen interest in writing.

The woman felt certain that her daughter would never make a decent living in the writing profession and tried to discourage her. She didn't tell the girl about the palm reader because she didn't want the child influenced by the prediction. Yet regardless of whatever else she tried to interest her daughter in, the child continued filling notebooks with poetry and essays.

When the girl entered college, her mother urged her to take up accounting. She tried it, but after just one term switched to an English and journalism major. Today she's a grown woman who has published over eighty-five books. A

A palm reader told Elaine Landau's mother that Elaine would turn out to be a writer. Maybe a palm reader told your mother that you would someday be a reader? You are, after all, reading one of Elaine Landau's books right now.

palm reader's prediction made before she was born had come to be.

I know this story is true because my mother is the woman who saw the palm reader and I'm the daughter who became a writer. But I don't know how a palmist who had never seen my mother before that day could have known my future. And I can't quite dismiss what happened as a coincidence. Like countless other predictions that came true, it remains a mystery.

Notes

Introduction
1. Felicia R. Lee, "Palms Read, Fortunes Told, But No Guarantees," *The New York Times* (July 7, 1993), p. B3.

Chapter One
1. The Editors of Time-Life Books, *Visions and Prophecies,* Mysteries of the Unknown series (Alexandria, Va.: Time-Life Books, 1988), p. 49.

Chapter Two
1. S. Lynn Chiger, "Your Destiny Is in Your Hands," *Mademoiselle* (June 1994), p. 153.

Chapter Three
1. Richard Cavendish, *Man, Myth & Magic: An Illustrated Encyclopedia of The Supernatural* (New York: Marshall Cavendish, 1970), p. 2794.

Chapter Five
1. Felicia R. Lee, p. B3.
2. Ibid.

Glossary

cobra—a poisonous snake found in Asia and Africa

crystal—a sometimes colorless transparent (see-through) rock that some believe has healing or cleansing properties

cue—a signal or sign

dupe—to purposely fool or mislead

goblet—a round long-stemmed drinking glass

inquirer—a person who seeks out the services of a fortune-teller

maintenance—keeping something in good working condition

organic—a naturally grown food

palmistry—the ancient art of seeing someone's future by reading his or her palm

prediction—forecast of a future event

restitution—returning or restoring something taken from someone

scrying—the centuries-old practice of seeing someone's future by focusing on a smooth clear object such as a crystal ball

tarot cards—a handsome deck of cards sometimes used for fortune-telling

vision—a mental picture of a person, place, or thing

Index

About the Author

Elaine Landau has written more
than eighty-five books for young
people and especially enjoys
researching new topics. Since writing
this book, she has tried to read her
own tea leaves on a number of occasions.
However, unable to come to any clear
conclusions, she may switch to coffee.

Ms. Landau lives in Sparta, New Jersey,
with her husband who only drinks orange juice
and a son who prefers milk.